Destined
for

LOVE

Marty Delmon

DESTINED FOR LOVE
Marty Delmon

Published by:
RPJ & COMPANY, INC.
P.O. Box 160243 | Altamonte Springs, FL 32716-0243 | 407.551.0734
www.rpjandco.com

All rights reserved. No part of this book may be reproduced or transmitted in any form or by any means, electronic or mechanical, including photocopying, recording, or by any information storage and retrieval system, without written permission from the author, except for the inclusion of brief quotations in a review. For information, please contact the publisher.

Copyright © 2010 by Marty Delmon

First printing
February 2010

ISBN-13: 978-0-9761122-9-7
ISBN-10: 0-9761122-9-9

Cover & Interior Layout & Design:
RPJ & Company, Inc.
www.rpjandco.com

Cover Image:
© Uschi Hering - Fotolia.com

Scripture taken from the New King James Version, unless otherwise noted. Copyright © 1982 by Thomas Nelson, Inc. Used by permission. All rights reserved.

Printed in the United States of America.

Destined for

LOVE

Marty Delmon

RPJ & Company, Inc.
www.rpjandco.com

Table of Contents

The Love of God .... page 1

The Love Commandment .... page 15

The Love Comportment.......... page 31

The Love Reward .... page 61

More Books .... page 78

A Message from the Author ..... page 88

THE LOVE OF GOD

In my early walk with the Lord I hastened to every anointed meeting I could find and especially looked for ones with good music that honored and loved God. One night, as I stood with all the others, my arms stretched toward Heaven, my body bristled with desire to let God know how much I loved Him. Singing my love from the depths of my being, suddenly I came to myself.

"Lord," I said, "how come I'm giving You all this love and I don't feel anything coming back to me? Here I am, my fingertips straining to caress You, my arms desperately reaching for You and my body swaying with the music in the delight of loving You. My love for You feels like a freight train rushing up from my toes and racing into Heaven to deliver carload after carload of love. And from You there is nothing. Why is that?"

I didn't change my posture; I simply stopped the flow of my love in order to listen to His answer. He said, "You could not be giving Me any love at all if I didn't first give My love to you."

I said, "So then You are pouring out Your love on me at the same time that I am sending my love to You?"

"Yes," He quietly said.

"Why don't I feel it?"

"Because you are focused on your love for Me."

I decided that I would then focus on His love coming to me and I looked for it. Rushing down from Heaven clamored this heavy-duty freight train of love that charged right through my body but when it got to my feet it didn't turn around and go back up to Him. It kind of crashed right there in my shoes.

I said, "What's this? Why did Your love just stop?"

He said, "My love goes in a circle. You have to keep on giving love in order for My love to flow through you.

That trainload of love is still chugging away, isn't it? It just doesn't have anywhere to go. If you will keep loving Me, My love will overwhelm you. You and I will be a continuous circle of love."

I returned to gushing my love on Him, and then I could feel His love being poured out on me. This was my first encounter with the fact that love is not a feeling; it's not even a decision. Love is a person. Love is God Almighty, love is Jesus Christ my Lord and love is the Holy Spirit, my guide and constant companion.

"He who does not love does not know God, for God is love" (1 John 4:8).

Notice this verse does not say God has love, or God gives love, or God creates love, or anything else that puts love a bit outside of Himself, like a tool or an emotion He might own. No, it says God is love. That's what He is made of. If that is who He is then we can turn that sentence around and say Love is God.

"God is love, and he who abides in love abides in God, and God in him. …because as He is, so are we in this world" (1 John 4:16b, 17b).

'Wait a minute,' I can hear you say, 'I'm just a human being. I can't be God. I can't be full of love all the time. Besides, how can He be made of love when I hear so much about His Wrath? What about Holy Anger? What about Judgment?'

The Bible does not say He is made of those things. Wrath, anger, judgment exist, but that's not who He is. Those are the emotions He has and the tools He uses from time to time, but He never stops loving you because love is who He is. He cannot stop being Himself anymore than you can stop being who you are.

He is a parent. Remember that. We call Him 'Father'. Here's what He says about His fatherhood.

"For whom the Lord loves He chastens, and scourges every son whom He receives" (Hebrews 12:6).

"As many as I love, I rebuke and chasten. Therefore be zealous and repent" (Revelation 3:19).

He's the model for earthly fathers: constant love, even when angry, even when giving judgment that the child needs a good spanking. Whenever the Lord has been angry with me He makes His accusation with such love I am brought to immediate repentance, but I first had to learn to trust the love He has for me.

Before you can make any inroads into receiving the love you're destined to receive, you must establish the reality of God's love for you, personally. Start with the most famous Scripture in the Bible.

"For God so loved the world that He gave His only begotten Son, that whoever believes in Him should not perish but have everlasting life" (John 3:16).

Let's face it, you were lost, you couldn't find your way to God even if you had a map (which you did have because it's in the Bible). Certain religions work really hard to please God so that they might, just might, get into Heaven when they die. Sorry to burst your bubble but it is impossible to do enough good to overcome the bad you also do.

Don't rear up angry with me and emphatically tell me what a good person you are. What about every evil thought you have, like behind the wheel of a car. Do you think loving thoughts about those who cut you off, or go slow in your lane, or flip you off because of the way you drive? If you were to count every thought and add them up, how many would be loving and how many would be non-loving?

Especially about yourself. What do you really think about yourself? Are you a boaster? Or do you demean yourself? Remember, you have to account for every idle thought. If the standard is God, that you be like Him, can you really call yourself good?

Knowing that only a blood covenant will bring you into His Glory, His Kingdom, God sent His Son to die for you so that His blood could be used to pay for your sins. How much love is that? A lot more than I have. You won't catch me sacrificing my son Jeff so that your sins can be paid for! Pay for your own sins!

"But God demonstrates His own love toward us, in that while we were still sinners, Christ died for us" (Romans 5:8).

"Greater love has no one than this, than to lay down one's life for his friends" (John 15:13).

This is such a well-known story that I think it loses its impact through its familiarity. So consider this: who would you die for? Would you die for your close-up loved ones? Would you die for a member of your church? Would you die for a stranger?

When I was married I had a dream. In this dream an enemy army lined up all the Christians in rows and rows, insisting we stand at attention. Then the general commanded my husband to stand in front of everyone and turn around so they could see his face.

He then shouted out over the enormous crowd of Christians, "Who will die in this man's place?" He waited. "No one? I thought you Christians were supposed to love each other so much you'd give up your life for a fellow Christian. I'll ask one more time and if no one comes forward I'm going to shoot him right in front of you."

No one moved a muscle. Standing in the front line I waited to see if anyone would take his place and no one did. There was absolute silence in all those ranks. Hesitantly, I took a step forward. That's when I woke up!

So who would you die for? Who would that general have to put in front of the ranks to cause you to step forward? To even contemplate such a monstrous thing as forfeiting your life, your existence, your breath, your blood flow, your heart beat, makes the reality of what God did extremely significant.

"But God, who is rich in mercy, because of His great love with which He loved us," (Ephesians 2:4).

God brought you back home to His arms by sacrificing His Son Jesus. Did He exchange one Son for another child? No. He still loves Jesus as much as ever. But He also loves you. Jesus was willing to obey His Father and to pay the price for your return and God was willing to sacrifice His Son in order to have you as a child.

"In this the love of God was manifested toward us, that God has sent His only begotten Son into the world, that we might live through Him" (1 John 4:9).

Through the love of God, demonstrated by the death, burial and resurrection of Jesus and through the love of Jesus that prompted Him to give up His life for you, you now have eternal life, Zoë life, agape life, everything good and wonderful. You, by the awesome act of Jesus Christ, and if you have accepted Him as your own Lord, have been adopted and are now a child of God and therefore heir of all the benefits of the Kingdom of Heaven.

The love children have for their parents sometimes astounds me. My little grandson, Alex, displays such passionate love for his mother it really ought to be captured on canvas. My three granddaughters, Brittany, Victoria and Madison, though teenagers, love their mother unconditionally. Those two mothers also love their children to the point of giving up their lives for them.

That's like you and God. He calls you His child, not out of obligation because He has to, but out of passionate love. You can count on it: HE LOVES YOU!

"Behold what manner of love the Father has bestowed on us, that we should be called children of God!" (1 John 3:1a).

It's not that you love Him like my grandchildren love their mothers; it's that He loves you and He dreamed up the way to save you from yourself, from your sins, and from your enemy, Satan.

"In this is love, not that we loved God, but that He loved us and sent His son to be the propitiation for our sins…. We love Him because He first loved us" (1 John 4:10, 19).

Get it fixed in your mind. God loves you. Jesus loves you. It doesn't matter what you did or what you did not do. You are loved by the Father and by the Son. The Holy Spirit lives inside you to lavish you with Their love. Yes, you could have murdered someone or lots of people and yes, They would still love you. Your repentance would put you immediately back in the presence of God. I appreciate very much the prayer in Ephesians.

"…that He would grant you, according to the riches of His glory, to be strengthened with might through His Spirit in the inner man, that Christ may dwell in your hearts through

faith; that you, being rooted and grounded in love, may be able to comprehend with all the saints what is the width and length and depth and height – to know the love of Christ which passes knowledge; that you may be filled with all the fullness of God" (Ephesians 3:16-19).

Just what do you think that fullness is? It's love. Remember? That's what He's made of! He is full of love! You can be full of love also by knowing God's love, which never, ever ends. Of course humans have disappointed you, even made you afraid to love and perhaps you have no hope of ever being loved. But God's love is divine! It's forever! We'll never know the full range of it!

I liked attending a Friday night Healing Service in the early days of my Christian life, and again, I attended because of the awesome music within which I poured my love out on God. But this particular night I decided it was time I went forward for prayer, even though physically nothing was wrong with me.

A certain woman assigned to pray for me asked what I wanted from the Lord. I said, "Ask Him to forgive me for being such an awful person." Now I really thought that. My mother convinced me of my worthlessness, my stepfather especially induced such thoughts, my husband also, well, just about everybody I could think of had this lowly opinion of me. That was my mind-set.

The woman started praying and stumbled to a stop. She said, "I can't pray that prayer for you. God thinks you are perfect just the way you are. Go home and read the book Song of Solomon in the Old Testament. That is a love letter written to you by God."

So I went home, got into my pajamas, crawled into bed and opened my Bible to Song of Solomon. I cried and cried and cried. It was impossible for anyone to love me with the kind of love I read about in those pages. I read that book every night before going to sleep and every night I cried.

During that time when I closed the Bible and turned out the light, I could feel the arms of Jesus wrapped around me rocking me to sleep. Finally after three months I stopped crying and accepted the love of God. Then after some years of pulling the devil's lies out of my soul and planting God's truth, my mind-set is now that everyone loves me, and I love everyone. Sometimes I need little on-the-spot adjustments, but I always come back to this conclusion: I am lovable and I love loving people.

"Who shall separate us from the love of Christ? Shall tribulation, or distress, or persecution, or famine, or nakedness, or peril, or sword? As it is written: 'For Your sake we are killed all day long; We are accounted as sheep for the slaughter.' Yet in all these things we are more than conquerors through Him who loved us. For I am persuaded that neither death nor life, nor angels nor principalities nor powers, nor things present nor things to come, nor height nor depth, nor any other created thing, shall be able to separate us from the love of God which is in Christ Jesus our Lord" **(Romans 8:35-39)**.

That love is mine. I've done nothing to deserve it; I've just given myself to God and I believe in His Son. So I have that love. Father God and Jesus Christ have an unprecedented love for each other. Their love is what I want to emulate. The Father watched over Jesus while He was here on the earth, told Him what to say, what to do, and guided His every move. Given the Holy Spirit in full measure, Jesus had all power and all authority yet He honored His Father to the extent He did nothing on His own accord. He only said what He heard His Father say and did what He saw His Father do. That level of trust singly comes from a profound love.

"But that the world may know that I love the Father, and as the Father gave Me commandment, so I do…." (John 14:31).

His Father loved Him to the magnitude that He could entrust Jesus with the task of paying for the sins of the world. He counted this one effort to perform the mission, and He knew He could rely on that effort because He and Jesus had such a magnificent love relationship. The Father loved Jesus so much He pronounced it from Heaven, which I'm sure disquieted more than a few people.

"And the Holy Spirit descended in bodily form like a dove upon Him, and a voice came from heaven which said, "You are My beloved Son; in You I am well pleased." (Luke 3:22).

Wouldn't you love to have that spoken over you? Now, after learning more and more about God's love, Jesus says that to me every day. Of course He doesn't say 'Son' He says 'You are My beloved.' Does He love you? What do you think? Jesus, Himself, loved you so much He came to earth prepared to die for you.

"I have come that they may have life, and that they may have it more abundantly. I am the good shepherd. The good shepherd gives His life for the sheep (John 10:10b, 11).

This massive sacrifice, putting Himself on the cross in your place and my place took more love than I can comprehend. In my natural life I have absolutely nothing to compare it with. I have observed families, couples, friends who have admirable love for each other, but they have no evidence like The Cross to demarcate their love. Nor do I. It's the ultimate love story.

One evening as I strolled around my living room lighting candles, praying in tongues under my breath, one candle burned me and another fell on my foot. So I stopped to see what was behind these actions.

As I listened the Lord said, "Sit down, I want to talk to you." So I sat. "Marty, I love you."

I said, "Yeah, I know."

He said, "No, you don't know. You don't know it through and through." Suddenly I had a little vision of my body partitioned into parts that I knew and parts that I didn't.

He said, "I want your body, your mind, your emotions and your will soaked in My love. Find Scriptures of My love and add them to your daily reading. Practice My love. When every move you make, every thought you think, every word you speak is saturated with My love, I will be able to use you as I please."

Of course being a completely surrendered vessel for His use is my heart's desire! I spend time just loving Him, making that circle flow, quoting the love Scriptures and thereby filling myself with His love. I've decided it's the most important thing I can do in my Christian walk. I spend whole evenings sometimes wrapping Him in my spiritual arms and being wrapped in His.

Therefore, I'm still dazed by how far I am from that goal, how easily I can lose my love. Here I am writing this book and today, in the line in the post office, some woman pushed in front of me. Could I let it go? No. I thought of all the things I could say to her to put her in her place. Fortunately, before I reached the postmistress I let it go. Jesus would have loved that woman until His love changed her. I chastised myself enough that Jesus didn't have to say a thing to me. I want to be full of love 100% of the time.

Jesus is. God is. I'm made in their image. I know it's a choice. I can be 100% love all the time. Jesus continued to love even to the moment everyone abandoned Him. Even to the last dregs of His life. He still loved.

"Now before the Feast of the Passover, when Jesus knew that His hour had come that He should depart from this world to the Father, having loved His own who were in the world, He loved them to the end" (John 13:1).

I can count on His love 100% of the time. How do I keep myself filled with His love? That goes right back to my original story. Round and round and round it goes; a circle of love. From the Father to me, to the Father, to me, to the Father, to me…. If I want love, I've got to give it away.

"…the love of God has been poured out in our hearts by the Holy Spirit who was given to us" (Romans 5:5b).

Can you see what to do with that love? It's not for you or me to wallow in. It's for you and me to give away and thereby keep a constant and refreshing flow of love washing through us. If you want love, you've got to give it away.

THE LOVE COMMANDMENT

When my son was a teenager, lo these 25 years ago, we lived in my dream house. I call it that because the Lord gave me a dream about this house before I saw it and the minute I opened the front door I saw exactly what He had shown me in the dream. We bought it immediately and we were happy there!

Built into a hillside, the front door opened onto the floor with the public rooms and the Master bedroom, but downstairs were three bedrooms, a game room and the back door opened out to the swimming pool.

On one school night, about two in the morning, I heard the television blaring in the kitchen/family room right outside my bedroom door. I went to see who was up and why they were watching TV! My son sat benignly on the couch in front of the set. I put one hand on my hip and with the other pointed strongly to the stairway.

"What are you thinking? This is a school night! Get back downstairs and go to bed!" He got up, never saying a word to me and disappeared down the stairs. Later, thinking about the turn of events, I wondered if he hadn't been sleep-walking and the Holy Spirit simply used him to bring me to the television set.

I turned from watching him go back to his bedroom, intending to turn the TV off when I noticed a film was just beginning. Movies easily capture my attention, so I sat down to see what was coming on. Definitely a grade B movie, but the story line caught me. A teen-age cheerleader, naturally the most popular girl in the high school, fell in love with the football hero, naturally the most popular boy in the high school.

She was rich. He was poor. The two families held such disdain for each other they knew their relationship would never be accepted, so they eloped. She gave up being a cheerleader. He gave up being a football star. She gave up college in an expensive Ivy League school. He gave up a football scholarship in a State college. She gave up her money. He gave up his potential of learning how to make money. All for their very passionate love for each other.

Like I said, it was grade B, so of course everyone reconciles in the end and the two are brought back home, their tuition to the local university is taken care of and they live happily ever after. Watching to the bitter end I clicked off the TV and went to bed. But I laid there steaming mad.

"No one ever gave up anything for me! Why is that, God? Why couldn't anyone have loved me enough to take care of me!?" I was more than mad; I wanted answers. So I waited for His response. In His typical fashion, instead of giving me straight forward answers, He asked me a question in return.

"Where's the love in you?"

Puzzled, I said, "I don't know."

"Look and see."

So I looked inside of myself. It was pitch black. I said, "I don't see any love in me."

He said, "Look again."

This time I looked harder and way deep down, somewhere in the very bottom of me I saw a tiny spark of red. "Well, I see maybe an ember, or a pilot light, or something red burning way down there."

He said, "Blow on it. Make it grow. Make it fill you up."

Marty Delmon

I did. I blew. I acted like a bellows and the red flame filled me up.

"Good." He said, "Love yourself. Now blow on it so it spreads to your husband."

This did not sit well with me. My husband was certainly one of the parties who had never given anything up for me. But, one does not waste an encounter with God, so I blew on the red coals until they also covered my husband.

"Good," God nodded. "Now blow until your love covers all the houses in your cul-de-sac."

I did that and it seemed the whole neighborhood burst into flame.

"Good," God encouraged, "Now blow until your love covers your whole town."

It didn't take as long as I thought it would. Soon my whole town sparkled bright red.

"Good," God continued, "Now blow until your love covers your whole state."

'Geez,' I thought, 'how much love is actually in me?' But I blew and soon all of California flickered and flamed.

"Good," God said matter-of-factly, "Now blow until your love covers your whole country."

At about this point I wanted to say, 'Hey, wait a minute. This is more than is humanly possible.' But I didn't. I continued to blow until the goal accomplished itself. However, God wasn't satisfied.

"Good," He smiled, "Now blow until your love covers the world."

I did and I covered the world with my love, my red, flaming, spark-shooting love.

"Very good," He said. "Now you go out and love the world and don't concern yourself with who loves you. I love you and it's My love you'll take to the world."

"Teacher, which is the great commandment in the law? Jesus said to him, You shall love the Lord your God with all your heart, with all your soul, and with all your mind. This is the first and great commandment. And the second is like it: You shall love your neighbor as yourself. On these two commandments hang all the Law and the Prophets" (Matthew 22:36-40).

Jesus is talking here about the commandments given in the Old Testament. The first is a commandment summarized from passages in Deuteronomy and the second comes from Leviticus 19:18. A very interesting thing happens between the Old Testament and the New. Readers of the Bible know that Jesus did not come to end the Law. He came to fulfill it. The Law will remain, not one jot or tittle will be removed, but in Jesus the Law is complete.

"For the commandments, 'You shall not commit adultery,' 'You shall not murder,' 'You shall not steal,' 'You shall not bear false witness,' 'You shall not covet,' and if there is any other commandment, are all summed up in this saying, namely, 'You shall love your neighbor as yourself.' Love does no harm to a neighbor; therefore love is the fulfillment of the law" (Romans 13:9-10).

When Jesus, the Son of God, came on the scene He gave a new law. Does that mean the old is obsolete? No. It means Jesus gave a higher commandment than was found in the old. Never does Jesus quarrel with the law or denounce it. But the old law is a spring board for the new law.

"As the Father loved Me, I also have loved you; abide in My love. If you keep My commandments, you will abide in My love, just as I have kept My Father's commandments and abide in His love. These things I have spoken to you, that My joy may remain in you and that your joy may be full. THIS IS MY COMMANDMENT, THAT YOU LOVE ONE ANOTHER AS I HAVE LOVED YOU" (John 15:9-12).

The commandments to love God with all your heart and to love your neighbor as yourself will never go away. Like Him telling me to love the entire world with His love. Let me **emphatically emphasize**, continuing to observe the law to love your neighbor as yourself is simply life; a life of love. Jesus is adding something to that command, however.

One morning I woke up unhappy. I don't like that feeling so I asked the Lord to show me the root of that. He immediately picked up a rock and written on that rock was the word 'Sadness'. (See my Buried Lies Companion Workbook to learn more about the prayer process we stepped into here.)

He turned the rock over and the lie written on the back side said, "Nobody will ever love me." He showed me certain events in my life which affirmed to me that nobody would ever love me. When we got to the root I asked the Lord for the truth for my life.

He explained it to me. He said I was loved by the greatest love in the world – His. But how could He get that love to me if I wouldn't let Him use my love? In other words, along with other ways, God loves me through my love for myself. My understanding was fuzzy until a certain woman in one of my workshops in France related this experience.

The Lord presented her with three people she needed to forgive. So she did. Then He said there was one more she needed to forgive. She asked, "Who?"

He said, "I'm looking at her."

In shock she asked, "Me?"

He nodded. Then she saw herself as if standing outside her body looking at herself. The Lord asked, "Do you love this woman?"

She said, "Yes, I suppose so."

"If you love this woman you can forgive her, can't you?"

She said yes. He said, "Then do it."

So she forgave herself and embraced herself in love and the two beings became one again.

When I heard this it clarified my own truth which is, "The greatest Lover in the world loves me through me." I, too, forgave myself for believing the lie that nobody will ever love me and acting as if it were true and now all those triggers of sadness are gone.

Without this step of loving yourself you cannot go on to what Jesus is now commanding you to do. Loving yourself is the same as loving someone else; you can't pretend its true, you can't work up a good façade, you have to honestly love yourself. But doesn't the Bible say you shouldn't think well of yourself? No, it says you mustn't think more highly of yourself than you ought. Christians think well of themselves without stepping over into pride.

"You are My friends if you do whatever I command you. These things I command you, that you love one another" (John 15:14, 17).

You may be scratching your head saying, 'I don't get it. Love yourself, love your neighbor, love one another. What's the difference? It's all the same commandment. There's no difference between the old and the new.'

Ah, but there is. And when you see it, the whole New Testament will take on a new light. As it stands today if you ask any believer what are the commandments he or she will respond to love God with all your heart and all your strength, etc., and to love your neighbor as yourself. Jesus only referred to those two commandments when He spoke about the law. His commandment is something altogether different.

"A new commandment I give to you, that you love one another; as I have loved you, that you also love one another. By this all will know that you are My disciples, if you have love for one another" (John 13:34-35).

Perhaps this will bring a little more punch to the understanding.

"Bear one another's burdens, and so fulfill the law of Christ" (Galatians 6:2).

What you are being commanded to do is known as the Law of Christ. The Old Testament Law is called the Royal Law.

"If you really fulfill the royal law according to the Scripture, 'You shall love your neighbor as yourself,' you do well;" (James 2:8).

But that is not the Law of Christ. That's Old Testament. Let's see if this will clarify it for you.

"He who says, 'I know Him,' and does not keep His commandments, is a liar, and the truth is not in him. But whoever keeps His word, truly the love of God is perfected in him. By this we know that we are in Him. He who says he abides in Him ought himself also to walk just as He walked. He who says he is in the light, and hates his brother, is in darkness until now. He who loves his brother abides in the light, and there is no cause for stumbling in him" (1 John 2:4-6, 9-10).

The Law of Christ is that you are to love your fellow brothers and sisters in Christ. You are to love the children of God, and who are they? They are the ones who receive Jesus as Lord. There are no others. When the world sees Christians loving each other they will be jealous of what the Christians have. They aren't jealous of your prosperity or even your health. They are jealous of your love.

Let's take one more look at the law.

"Then one of the scribes came, and having heard them reasoning together, perceiving that He had answered them well, asked Him, "Which is the first commandment of all?" Jesus answered him, "The first of all the commandments is: 'Hear, O Israel, the LORD our God, the LORD is one. And you shall love the LORD your God with all your heart, with all your soul, with all your mind, and with all your strength.' This is the first commandment. And the second, like it, is

this: 'You shall love your neighbor as yourself.' There is no other commandment greater than these." So the scribe said to Him, "Well said, Teacher. You have spoken the truth, for there is one God, and there is no other but He. And to love Him with all the heart, with all the understanding, with all the soul, and with all the strength, and to love one's neighbor as oneself, is more than all the whole burnt offerings and sacrifices. Now when Jesus saw that he answered wisely, He said to him, "You are not far from the kingdom of God." But after that no one dared question Him" (Mark 12:28-34).

The Law of the Old Testament does not get a person into the Kingdom of God. This man had the Old Law down pat, but he wasn't in the Kingdom. Why not? Number one, he didn't have Jesus as His Lord and the Bible says that no one comes to the Father except through the Son. And number two, there was therefore a new law of love to follow. No longer is the law to love the world, your neighbor, whoever needs your help, no matter what their belief. Note carefully, Christians are to continue to practice this commandment, only now they have a higher commandment. Now the Law of Christ charges you to love your fellow believer, your sibling in the family of God, the other children, the younger brothers and sisters of Jesus Christ.

"…since we heard of your faith in Christ Jesus and of your love for all the saints;" (Colossians 1:4).

Notice what draws Paul's attention beyond their faith in Jesus – their love for all the saints. The saints are the believers and followers of Jesus.

"Whoever believes that Jesus is the Christ is born of God, and everyone who loves Him who begot also loves him who is begotten of Him. By this we know that we love the children of God, when we love God and keep His commandments. For this is the love of God, that we keep His commandments. And His commandments are not burdensome" (1 John 5:1-3).

His commandment is that we love the children of God, that we love each other.

"Beloved, let us love one another, for love is of God; and everyone who loves is born of God and knows God. Beloved, if God so loved us, we also ought to love one another. No one has seen God at any time. If we love one another, God abides in us, and His love has been perfected in us" (1 John 4:7, 11-12).

This perfection of love seems to be a major issue to Jesus. We ought to focus on loving one another as in this way the love of Jesus is perfected in us. In fact, I would say the Church has greatly missed its calling in this arena. We pay little attention to our fellow believers' needs. We put the world before the church, but that's not how Jesus wants it. He loves His own first.

Think of the feeding programs, the clothing programs, the building programs the church has for the poor. It seems noble, doesn't it? At the same time I've noticed a bit of disdain toward anyone in the church who has trouble providing for their family or even for themselves. There's always muttering about how that person is outside of the will of God. Or that he or she made her bed (it's his or her fault) so they should just lie in it.

Christians are put into families as an example of how to be in a church. You provide for your family first. Then you take care of others. You don't feed someone else your children's food, or your aging parents' food. If you do feed others first the Bible calls you "worse than an infidel." The ONLY exception is if God, Himself, has asked you for a sacrificial gift which will open the door for a great blessing.

What does it do to us to put things in the right perspective? To follow that commandment to love one another?

"Now the purpose of the commandment is love from a pure heart, from a good conscience, and from sincere faith," (1 Timothy 1:5).

Is Paul saying that loving your fellow brothers and sisters in Christ is a purifier? That the effort it will take to love these rascals will purify your heart, purify your conscience and bring you down to the basics of sincere faith? Probably so. I know I sometimes want to say right out to people who can't seem to get it right, "Shape up! Get with the program! Do what Jesus tells you to do and you'll have plenty!"

I don't know how many Christians tell me they'd rather do business with the unsaved than with their fellow believers. Christians have a reputation for being disappointing businessmen, not doing what they say, not showing up for appointments, begging off work because of this complaint or that difficulty. So honest folk tend not to want to deal with them. Yet here's what Jesus says about it.

"Yet it shall not be so among you; but whoever desires to become great among you shall be your servant. And whoever of you desires to be first shall be slave of all. For even the Son of Man did not come to be served, but to serve, and to give His life a ransom for many" (Mark 10:43-45).

It's much easier to love the world than to love our own brothers and sisters in Christ. When you look at the world you can just say, 'Oh well, Father, forgive them because they don't know what they're doing.' Whereas a believer, when they make the same blunder, does know what they're doing and it is most annoying. However, your job is to serve the contrary Christian who is causing you delay, or whatever the difficulty. You, by seeing him or her through to the end of the job, can help them become better more efficient Christians.

You aren't given the leeway to deal with the world and ignore the family of God. Loving each other is a commandment, not a suggestion. It is, in fact, the only commandment of Jesus Christ.

"Just as He chose us in Him before the foundation of the world, that we should be holy and without blame before Him in love," (Ephesians 1:4).

"If you love Me, keep My commandments" (John 14:15).

THE LOVE COMPORTMENT

"And being in Bethany at the house of Simon the leper, as He sat at the table, a woman came having an alabaster flask of very costly oil of spikenard. Then she broke the flask and poured it on His head. But there were some who were indignant among themselves, and said, 'Why was this fragrant oil wasted? For it might have been sold for more than three hundred denarii and given to the poor.' And they criticized her sharply. But Jesus said, 'Let her alone. Why do you trouble her? She has done a good work for Me. For you have the poor with you always, and whenever you wish you may do them good; but Me you do

not have always. She has done what she could. She has come beforehand to anoint My body for burial. Assuredly, I say to you, wherever this gospel is preached in the whole world, what this woman has done will also be told as a memorial to her'" (Mark 14:3-9).

Well, wasn't she the special one! I mean, she happened to be alive when Jesus walked the earth. If I'd been alive it might be me that would be mentioned as a memorial. Or you. But we missed our chance because of a bad birth date! Or did we? Jesus went on to explain.

"Then the King will say to those on His right hand, 'Come, you blessed of My Father, inherit the kingdom prepared for you from the foundation of the world: for I was hungry and you gave Me food; I was thirsty and you gave Me drink; I was a stranger and you took Me in; I was naked and you clothed Me; I was sick and you visited Me; I was in prison and you came to Me. Then the righteous will answer Him, saying, 'Lord, when did we see You hungry and feed You, or thirsty and give You drink? When did we see You a stranger and take You in, or naked and clothe You? Or when did we see You sick, or in prison, and come to You? And the King will answer and say to them, 'Assuredly, I say to you, inasmuch as you did it to one of the least of these My brethren, you did it to Me.'" (Matthew 25:34-40).

Okay, maybe we have time after all. Maybe there is a memorial written for each of us as we follow those instructions. I know one couple who for sure have a memorial. I take people's testimonies so I can write up stories for the radio. I couldn't help but simply shake my head when I heard this one.

A certain couple asked the Lord who He would have them help in the Body of Christ. He gave them a name that had been reported in the newspapers for some months, a boy of 16 who cold-bloodedly took a cast iron skillet and whacked his father on the head, cracking his skull and killing him. Because of the heinous crime the boy, Darrell, was tried as an adult. During the trial he stopped talking and had not uttered a word since. At this moment he was incarcerated in the county jail awaiting the sentencing. Without question he would no doubt be sent to a federal prison.

The couple, Bruce and Cindy, went to the jail for a visit. The guards ushered the boy into the visiting room and he just sat there, staring at the floor. They were with him for one hour; he never looked at them nor responded to their questions. They were able to make two more visits before the authorities transferred him to a federal prison a few hours away. He still did not speak.

Once the boy was gone, the local police, seeing the sincerity in Bruce and Cindy, shared his file with them. Darrell's father, before being sent to eternity by a skillet, had been a pastor. His son, his only child, received Jesus as his Lord at the age of eight. From that moment on, the father gave the boy a rigorous training to develop his Christian character.

Everyday after school he chained him to a tree in the back yard. Regardless of weather, light, dark, warm, cold, rain, lightning, hail, snow, sleet, ice, Darrell stayed chained to that tree till 8 p.m. without jacket, water or food. No grass grew under that tree in the circumference of the chain as the boy ate it all.

The next door neighbors, who reported this after the murder, refused to testify out of fear of the church. If the pastor behaved in this manner, what might his parishioners do to them if they heard them in court? So the police could do nothing with this testimony.

For two years Bruce and Cindy drove the two hours each way to visit Darrell in the federal prison. Not once in the two years did he look at them or speak to them. Then he was moved to another prison in another state.

I would have been out of there when they moved him from jail to prison. Hey! If he won't talk to me, send somebody else in there. Not Bruce and Cindy; they just wouldn't quit. Because this new location required an airline flight and an overnight in a hotel, they only visited every other week, but that way they saw him two days in a row. When they came for their first visit in this prison, Darrell did look at them in surprise. From that point he scrutinized them on every visit.

Finally after another year, he spoke. Can you imagine persevering for three years before someone will even speak to you? I was humbled by this story. My patience is puny in comparison to this couple. I hold them up as Christian heroes!

Ten years later the petitions Bruce and Cindy continuously made to the warden were heard and the prison released Darrell on parole in the custody of his two, and only, faithful friends. By the time I got this story the young man, now 30, lived with Bruce and Cindy, had a solid job, and had met a lovely Christian woman at church. My story hasn't been aired on the radio yet, but I called it "Visiting Jesus in Prison."

Do you know how many Christians are in prison? A lot. Who visits them? Not many. I had the privilege of doing one of my workshops in an Orlando jail with women who were being held until a court date or a sentencing came up. Out of four living pods holding 100 prisoners each, they made one pod a Christian dormitory. 100 Christians in one Women's jail! Amazing. Calculate what that means across the United States.

The following year when I returned to Orlando, one of the Chaplains had started a ministry for women coming out of jail or prison. Most go right back to the life they had before, selling themselves to buy drugs. What these women need is someone to adopt them, individually, and help them to become all they can be. Chaplain Peg at Open Doors is working on that angle. Where are the Christians to do this? Hopefully those who are there will be as faithful as Bruce and Cindy.

"If I then, your Lord and Teacher, have washed your feet, you also ought to wash one another's feet. For I have given you an example, that you should do as I have done to you" *(John 13:14-15).*

Christianity is first an inward work. The New Testament teaches us how to change the inside through forgiveness and replacing lies we believe with the truth God teaches us to believe. After that Christianity is an outward work. We love, help and make disciples out of others. The very first ones we deal with are our fellow Christians. But what can we do for them?

"Then fear came upon every soul, and many wonders and signs were done through the apostles. Now all who believed were together, and had all things in common, and sold their possessions and goods, and divided them among all, as anyone had need" (Acts 2:43-45).

Why would they do such a preposterous thing? At no other time in history has the Church of Jesus operated like this. How could they trust the people they gave their life savings to, or love their fellow believers enough to sell their property to supply other people's needs? I've never even seen a hint of this in the church.

I have heard Pastors say this giving lifestyle failed because it was not God's will. Or did it fail because it was not man's will? We are the ones who choose to live according to our willingness to obey.

"Now the multitude of those who believed were of one heart and one soul; neither did anyone say that any of the things he possessed was his own, but they had all things in common. And with great power the apostles gave witness to the resurrection of the Lord Jesus. And great grace was upon

them all. Nor was there anyone among them who lacked; for all who were possessors of lands or houses sold them, and brought the proceeds of the things that were sold, and laid them at the apostles' feet; and they distributed to each as anyone had need" (Acts 4:32-35).

If this is the second mention of this kind of sharing activity, that means it is God's will. By two or three witnesses a thing is established, according to the Bible. Frankly, it's because Christians don't share with one another that makes us look like the world. We're just as greedy and hoarding as they are. They set the standard and we live up to it. It should be the other way around. The fallen world should not affect us; we should affect the fallen world.

"Be kindly affectionate to one another with brotherly love, in honor giving preference to one another; not lagging in diligence, fervent in spirit, serving the Lord; rejoicing in hope, patient in tribulation, continuing steadfastly in prayer; distributing to the needs of the saints, given to hospitality" (Romans 12:10-13).

Oops! A third witness! "Distributing to the needs of the saints!" What are we going to do with that? Notice the phrase 'given to hospitality.' Because I travel so much by car across the United States, speaking in churches, doing workshops, selling my books, I am delighted to have as a resource a catalog called, "Mennonite Your Way." Mennonite Christians believe hospitality pleases God, so they create a catalog every year with the names and addresses of Christians who will open their homes for travelers.

My catalog is eight years old and tattered as I stay in these homes as often as I can. For a pittance they will give me a bedroom with fresh sheets, a fluffy towel and for a few shekels more they'll feed me. They open up their lives to me and I think I go there more for the stories I hear than I do for a clean, fresh stay.

I've been in dozens of these homes and so far have yet to be in one where they did not have an adopted child. They go to the State and offer to adopt the unadoptable children. I've met deaf children, crippled children, blind children, but the most unforgettable child was a young woman in college.

Her adoptive parents had just completed an apartment downstairs so that she could have her independence and still stay home while she took her university classes. She can live adequately being semi on her own, but she's only recently arrived at the place where she can cope well; where she can function in life. She's only recently accepted their unconditional love for her.

When she first came to them she was six. Her "mothers" were in court to separate their affairs, a divorce if you will, and neither one wanted the child so the judge called this couple and asked them to adopt her. The first night she stayed in her adoptive home the girl would not go to bed. The husband and wife finally had to physically pick her up and put her in bed and the living nightmare began.

For years this wonderful Mennonite family had to force the child into bed and hold her down until she fell asleep from the utter exhaustion of the physical struggle she put them through. She was a teenager before she confided in them that her "mothers" molested her every night when they put her to bed. She'd had six years of this atrocious treatment in those delicate, formative years.

The wife of this couple asked me, "Where are the other Christians? As far as I know, only Mennonites do this kind of work for the Lord."

I wanted to say, "Maybe only the Mennonites are true Christians," but if I'd said that I would have had to include myself in the faulty part. I could have been a foster parent. I could have taken abandoned seniors out of the State home nearby for weekly outings. Why didn't I? The only reason I can think of is – I was too selfish.

"Therefore show to them, and before the churches, the proof of your love and of our boasting on your behalf" (2 Corinthians 8:24).

"For you, brethren, have been called to liberty; only do not use liberty as an opportunity for the flesh, but through love serve one another" (Galatians 5:13).

"...just as He chose us in Him before the foundation of the world, that we should be holy and without blame before Him in love," (Ephesians 1:4).

What does it mean to be without blame? No longer sinning? Keeping your nose clean? Avoiding the appearance of evil?

I believe being without blame means proving your love before the church body. It means serving one another through love. It means everyone can see your sacrifice of time, talent and finances for your brothers and sisters in Christ, not because you show it off but because it's evident. There's more.

"Let all bitterness, wrath, anger, clamor, and evil speaking be put away from you, with all malice. And be kind to one another, tenderhearted, forgiving one another, even as God in Christ forgave you" (Ephesians 4:31-32).

I don't know about you, but my brothers and sisters in Christ are the hardest ones for me to forgive. I have a gorgeous, vivacious, loving daughter named Jolie. There is a woman in her church who can't stand her, I think basically she's jealous, and she gossips about my daughter throughout the church, which I have such a hard time forgiving. This woman knows better!

Now my daughter has no problem at all. She forgives her and she loves her all the time. In certain cases like this I have to work really hard at forgiveness. I can pretty readily forgive offenses against me, but when it's my child, or my grandchild being persecuted, watch out! When I say that woman knows better I can say that with certainty because the New Testament is full of how to treat our brothers and sisters in Christ!

"Therefore if there is any consolation in Christ, if any comfort of love, if any fellowship of the Spirit, if any affection and

mercy, fulfill my joy by being like-minded, having the same love, being of one accord, of one mind. Let nothing be done through selfish ambition or conceit, but in lowliness of mind let each esteem others better than himself. Let each of you look out not only for his own interests, but also for the interests of others" (Philippians 2:1-4).

Let me be quick here to say that esteeming others better than yourself does not mean a Christian is a doormat. It does not mean you choose to listen to the lies of the devil in your regard and therefore believe that you are a lesser human being. You're not. You're the apple of God's eye. Choosing to esteem others better than yourself means to focus your attention on them instead of yourself and only see the wonderful things about them.

"But above all these things put on love, which is the bond of perfection" (Colossians 3:14).

So, if we want to be perfect, we have to order our relationships with God's children so that we are looking out for their interests. Loving them is the bond of perfection.

"And may the Lord make you increase and abound in love to one another and to all, just as we do to you," (1 Thessalonians 3:12).

I hope you are getting the picture. God wants us to be lovers of each other, first. Then be lovers of the world. The Church does it the other way around, first reaching the unsaved and if anything is left over the church might use it for the members. I would suggest a more radical point of view, one that puts Christians in harmony with Scripture. Ask the Lord to give you another believer to help and ask Him what to do for that person. What He tells you will be radical because He will require action on your part. Just do it.

Above all, be loving to your brothers and sisters in Christ. That doesn't mean that on Sunday mornings you come to Church well-dressed: for their benefit of course, with a bright smile: to spread good cheer, and nice things to say to people's faces. But then you go home and for one week not one of your siblings in Christ hears a word from you and you never dirty your hands by doing something for them.

Nor am I suggesting you make your Tuna Surprise Casserole and carry it to various people in your church. I can remember as a little girl listening to the women in my grandmother's hair salon brag to each other about how many casseroles of food they had distributed that week. There was a time when people did that.

Serving God is not brag time. Serving God is gratitude time. Thank God you get to do what He asks you to do because nothing is more rewarding. I'll get to that in the next chapter. If we really want God's blessings, then we will keep His commandments: Love One Another! And if you think you're doing enough, do more!

"And may the Lord make you increase and abound in love to one another and to all, just as we do to you" (1 Thessalonians 3:12).

"But concerning brotherly love you have no need that I should write to you, for you yourselves are taught by God to love one another; and indeed you do so toward all the brethren who are in all Macedonia. But we urge you, brethren, that you increase more and more;" (1 Thessalonians 4:9-10).

"We are bound to thank God always for you, brethren, as it is fitting, because your faith grows exceedingly, and the love of every one of you all abounds toward each other," (2 Thessalonians 1:3).

"And let us consider one another in order to stir up love and good works" (Hebrews 10:24).

When was the last time you heard of a wealthy church adopting a poor church and making sure that everyone in the poor church owns their own home and a good working car? Our government has tried to do this with disastrous results. You know why? That's not the job God assigned to governments. He assigned that to His own people to do for His own people.

Anytime a government tries to do what the Bible tells God's people to do, it fails and it usually fails miserably. A government worker who is working for pay will not do the job that a servant of God will do who is working for love.

A woman I knew had a massive stroke that left her paralyzed, unable to speak and she was placed in a government facility. Some other women and I went to visit. During that visit the woman had a bowel movement in her diaper, so we pushed the call button for a nurse. She came only after we pushed that button dozens of times.

Looking at the clock on the wall she said, "I changed her diaper at 8 a.m. and she's not scheduled for another diaper change until noon." With that she turned around and left the room. It was 10 a.m. We changed the woman's diaper. Heaven knows what that woman lived through for the rest of the time she spent in that facility. No one taking care of her loved her.

Let's be honest. We didn't change that diaper because we loved that woman either. We changed that diaper because we love God and He orders us to love that woman or whoever else He sends us to. Love is an action word; it's a verb. We 'do' love.

"Since you have purified your souls in obeying the truth through the Spirit in sincere love of the brethren, love one another fervently with a pure heart," (1 Peter 1:22).

"Honor all people. Love the brotherhood. Fear God. Honor the king" (1 Peter 2:17).

"Finally, all of you be of one mind, having compassion for one another; love as brothers, be tenderhearted, be courteous;" (1 Peter 3:8).

You may think I'm trying to cram the entire New Testament into this book. I just want you to see the focused attention the Word gives to loving your brothers and sisters in Christ. The Church seems to think that if it is courteous, that's enough. It isn't even the tip of the iceberg.

"And walk in love, as Christ also has loved us and given Himself for us, an offering and a sacrifice to God for a sweet-smelling aroma, speaking to one another in psalms and hymns and spiritual songs, singing and making melody in your heart to the Lord, giving thanks always for all things to God the Father in the name of our Lord Jesus Christ, submitting to one another in the fear of the Lord" (Ephesians 5:2, 19-20).

"How is it then, brethren? Whenever you come together, each of you has a psalm, has a teaching, has a tongue, has a revelation, has an interpretation. Let all things be done for edification" (1 Corinthians 14:26).

I'll never forget the first time this happened to me. One night, sitting in a restaurant, as I cut into my food with my fork, I heard a woman coming toward me singing under her breath. I had just put the fork in my mouth when she passed behind my chair and dipped her shoulder down to touch mine as she sang a prophetic word into my ear. That word changed my life and yet I never saw the woman's face because she continued on her way.

You know, Christians can identify each other in a crowd. It's spirit calling to spirit. Anyone who is born again has the Spirit of God living inside of them. Of course the Spirit recognizes the Spirit in someone else. And isn't that who we are loving when we love our brothers and sisters? Jesus in them? Doesn't that make the circle complete? God loves you, you love Jesus in someone else and Jesus loves the Father. Round and round and round it goes!

I did one of my prayer processes (from Buried Lies and Buried Lies Companion Workbook) after I had a run-in with a Christian brother who stole from me and tried to cover the theft by besmirching my name. However, no one believed him so he left the church in a huff. I went home and did my prayer process. The issue was: Men. The lie I believed was: All men are (to spare innocent eyes I'll use the word 'jerks'). I had good reason to believe this. My step-father raped me repeatedly and my former husband married me to hide his homosexuality.

The Lord showed me all kinds of events in my life where the men certainly acted like jerks. At the root I asked for the truth. Jesus appeared to me and said, "I am a man. I am not a jerk. Look for me in all men." I started doing that and you know what? He's there! Even if they are acting like jerks, Jesus is in the heart of every Christian and for those who aren't Christians yet, He is hovering above their heart waiting for the invitation to come in. That was the day men stopped being my adversaries. They're just people; people that Jesus loves.

"For this is the message that you heard from the beginning, that we should love one another.... Whoever hates his brother

is a murderer, and you know that no murderer has eternal life abiding in him. By this we know love, because He laid down His life for us. And we also ought to lay down our lives for the brethren. But whoever has this world's goods, and sees his brother in need, and shuts up his heart from him, how does the love of God abide in him? My little children, let us not love in word or in tongue, but in deed and in truth" (1 John 3:11, 15-18).

When I look back over my life, the things that have been the most memorable, outside of my direct, personal relationship with Jesus, have been the times when I made a distinct gifting of money to other children of God. I've made certain gifts to the church, but that didn't mean as much as what I am going to relate here.

One time a woman in my church needed a semester's tuition paid or she would have to drop out of the university. I paid it without telling her and I got the university to keep it a secret as well. A few weeks later, at a dinner party, this woman wept as she told the dinner guests how much that gift meant to her. I wept too, but not till I got home. What a privilege to give where God wanted me to give. I felt like I had received the prize.

Another time the Lord told me to help a certain man whom I did not know to start an audio lending library. I was on my way to visit my aunt in the foothills of California. I said, "Okay, Lord, but I'm not going to mention this to anyone. If this is You, You'll arrange for me to meet this man."

My aunt and I spent a nice weekend together with no word from the Lord about His project. When we entered my aunt's church – they were meeting in the public school as their building was in the process of being built – a man came out of a room across the entry hall. He strode right for me extending his hand to shake mine and welcome me to my aunt's church.

The words that came out of my mouth shocked me. I said, "Are you the one who wants to start an audio lending library?"

He acted like I had struck him, staggering back while he nodded, "Yes."

I said, "The Lord told me to give you the equipment you need to get the library started." He made sure I had his name and address before I left the church!

Back home I found a ministry that sold recording equipment for wholesale price and I was able to buy everything, brand new and of high quality, that the man could possibly want. When I received everything I piled it in the car and drove back up to the foothills to deliver it. I hadn't told my aunt, or anyone else, of this project.

When I drove up to the address I found myself in front of a ramshackle building about to fall down. Surely the Lord did not want this shiny, new equipment in this shabby building! But I took it in. The man was waiting for me and he showed me around. He ran a Christian coffee shop in the leaning-to-the-wind building and the week before he had led the regional drug lord to Jesus and the local drug ring had been destroyed.

He showed me his brochure which advertised an audio lending library. He said, "I wrote that in faith."

I can still remember, some 28 years later, exactly how I felt that day. Exhilarated would not be a strong enough word. God used me to accomplish His purposes! God used me to fulfill someone's faith! I got to be a part of God's plan, directly! It was total satisfaction, spirit, soul and body.

The biggest gift I ever gave was the down payment for a house for a Police Chaplain. He had been a professional golfer and made good money on the course. But the Lord redirected his life to ride in police cars and counsel the officers, to help them stabilize their lives through the daily trauma they experienced handling difficult situations. His pay hardly kept his family alive; a sharp decline for a winning golfer.

By the time I came into the picture he and his family lived in a drafty wooden building, an old henhouse or something. He wouldn't let me inside because he was so ashamed over where he lived. When the Lord told me to give him the down payment I could definitely see the need. However, I had never done anything so big. It took a giant step of obedience to let go of that much money at one time.

I don't remember ever seeing anybody more stunned than he was when I offered the down payment. That's pretty much how I felt inside; I, too, was stunned but I didn't let on. He and his wife found the prettiest house to buy and the whole transaction was an absolute joy!

When I came on the mission field, I had to get rid of a crew cab truck and a fifth wheel recreational vehicle. I thoroughly enjoyed those two as we traveled in them as a family and were so cozy inside. I wanted to keep them in storage, but my husband didn't want to pay the monthly bill. We prayed and the Lord told us to give the truck and the fifth wheeler to a certain ministry who itinerated. I cried when I let go of these two!

They, however, were thrilled. They put 200,000 miles on that truck and were able to take their family wherever they went. That was so much better than having my truck and trailer sit and rust. Besides, my kids told me they had outgrown that form of travel and they were glad it was gone. So God worked all things together for good for me who loves the Lord and am called according to His purpose.

I'm only writing these things to encourage you and myself. You who have the world's goods are required to share them with those in the Body of Christ who don't have the world's goods.

Did I lay down my life for my brethren? No. I'm the one who benefited. I've never stretched myself enough to actually call it laying down my life. I hope I have the courage to do that with the days I have left. I, like you, want to love in more and more deeds.

Right now my income comes from people giving to my missionary fund or from the purchase of my books. However, I give away more books than I sell. Why do I do this? The Lord tells me to give them away. I, of course, have to buy the books from my publisher, so it costs me to give them away. But peoples' lives are changed by what they read. Once more I have the privilege of playing a part in God's plan.

"But I say to you who hear: Love your enemies, do good to those who hate you, bless those who curse you, and pray for those who spitefully use you. To him who strikes you on the one cheek, offer the other also. And from him who takes away your cloak, do not withhold your tunic either. Give to everyone who asks of you. And from him who takes away your goods do not ask them back. And just as you want men to do to you, you also do to them likewise. But if you love those who love you, what credit is that to you? For even sinners love those who love them. And if you do good to those who do good to you, what credit is that to you? For even sinners do the same. And if you lend to those from whom you hope to receive back, what credit is that to you? For even sinners lend to sinners to receive as much back. But love your enemies, do good, and lend, hoping for nothing in return; and your reward will be great, and you will be sons of the Most High. For He is kind to the unthankful and evil. Therefore be merciful, just as your Father also is merciful. Judge not, and you shall not be judged. Condemn not, and you shall not be condemned. Forgive, and you will be forgiven. Give, and it will be given to you: good measure, pressed down, shaken together, and running over will be put into your bosom. For with the same

measure that you use, it will be measured back to you" (Luke 6:27-38).

My biggest enemies have always been in the church. I've rarely been persecuted by the world—certain unsaved members of my family make the exception—but I certainly have been lambasted by God's children. Because I'm a missionary the offenses have come along the lines of my work in France. I won't tell you my failures in dealing with these things; there's no glory in the failures except that I did get up and I kept going.

Let me tell you about a significant one in that the Lord changed something in me and I know from now on I'll be able to love my enemies and give them whatever they ask for. For several years while I established my radio ministry I attended a certain church where I only did things like act as greeter at the front door on Sunday mornings, and I cleaned the church on Saturdays. Then I returned to the States to spend several years raising money for the radio ministry.

When I returned to France the old pastor moved out of the country. The new pastor let me know he didn't want me to come back to the church. That didn't bother me too much as my denomination, Pentecostal Holiness, is close to the Church of God, and I intended to attend the new Church of God in town. The other church, in my absence, chose to be a Seeker Sensitive Church which means taking the Blood of Jesus and the Gifts of the Holy Spirit out of the doctrine. I knew I couldn't live with that.

However, I had made many friends in the old church and they were upset that I was not welcome in their church. I also attended their house group which kept our friendship going. They barraged the new pastor for two years wanting him to allow me to attend.

One day he called. He invited me to a meeting with him and his associate pastor. I assumed they were going to tell me I would be more than welcome to come back. They, however, told me they didn't want me to ever attend their church, not even for big public meetings where they had to rent a hall. They told me to stop attending the house group and not to allow any of their members to take my workshop. They finished by telling me not to associate with any of their members.

I was shocked. I asked the pastor, "What on earth do you have against me?"

He said, "Absolutely nothing. It is just a conviction of my heart."

I went home and quietly had a temper tantrum, just me in front of God. "How can You allow Your children to treat me like this? They need to be punished!!!!!" Suddenly I realized their words had no affect on my life. Our little meeting didn't change a thing. I'm still in France; I'm still serving God; He's still on the throne of my heart. What difference did it make?

The Lord asked me to give them everything they wanted. So I did. I invited my friends to my house for a dinner and explained why this would be our last time together. No more house group. No more socializing. They blustered a bit, but in the end they quietly agreed I was doing the right thing according to the Bible.

"You have heard that it was said, 'You shall love your neighbor and hate your enemy,' But I say to you, love your enemies, bless those who curse you, do good to those who hate you, and pray for those who spitefully use you and persecute you, that you may be sons of your Father in heaven; for He makes His sun rise on the evil and on the good, and sends rain on the just and on the unjust. For if you love those who love you, what reward have you? Do not even the tax collectors do the same? And if you greet your brethren only, what do you do more than others? Do not even the tax collectors do so? Therefore you shall be perfect, just as your Father in heaven is perfect" (Matthew 5:43-48).

Perfection. Can a person really achieve that? This verse looks to me like we are being commanded to be perfect. So it must be possible. What does being perfect mean? It means to be mature, grown-up, capable of living a life of equilibrium. Following Jesus in every domain of our lives.

A dear friend of mine, Daniel, was born and raised in Rwanda. However, before things got bad in that country the Lord told his father to move the family to Kenya, which he did. When the massacres happened some of Daniel's extended family were slaughtered, not to mention multitudes of friends and acquaintances.

One day Daniel visited Macon in northern France and went to the supermarket about one in the afternoon not realizing the shops kept the old hours that used to be popular throughout the country. They closed between noon and 2 p.m. Sitting in a circle by the door to the market were five men and their dogs.

These groups have suddenly sprung up all over France, disenchanted, disowned, mostly white, all ages, slovenly, men who shout and curse at those passing by. They have a mangy dog on a leash because the police cannot arrest them if they have a dog.

Daniel decided to wait the hour for the market to open as he felt urged by the Holy Spirit to talk to these five men. He sauntered over to them. "Mind if I join you?"

"Wow, not at all, sit down man. Somebody like you never comes to talk to us." Daniel looks, acts and talks like a professional athlete. He had, in fact, spent time on the tennis circuit but when it didn't 'happen' for him by his 25th year, he gave it up and went into business.

They offered him a beer which he declined. He asked what they were talking about and they replied the subject was love. All of them had been wounded in various affairs and were bemoaning the fact that such a wonderful feeling could be so easily smashed by such an awful feeling.

Daniel said, "But love is not a feeling."

"Hey, come on, man, that's all it is."

"No, love is a decision."

"What do you mean?"

"I'm from Rwanda and when people I loved were slaughtered I chose to forgive and to love those who killed them. I decided that. You're right, it felt good to decide that, but the feeling didn't come first, the decision came first."

Three of the men burst into tears. Two of which were sobbing. The milder one said, "We were in the French army in Rwanda. We've all killed. We could probably be the ones who killed the people you loved. We were innocent little kids. Yeah, we know we were under orders. Even so, how is God ever going to forgive us and love us again?"

This, of course, was the opening Daniel was sent there to walk into and he led all five men to Jesus and they received Him as their Lord. He gave them his phone number and they call from time to time with such wonderful reports of what Jesus is doing in their lives. One of them has a grandfather who, when he saw the change, transferred his factory in China to him and gave him an apartment building.

What's the change that people can see? It's love. Love perfects us. When I got born again I didn't realize how much my new birth had changed me until I heard my eleven year old daughter on the phone with a friend. "You should see my Mom! She's so different! She really loves me!"

"Then He also said to him who invited Him, 'When you give a dinner or a supper, do not ask your friends, your brothers, your relatives, nor rich neighbors, lest they also invite you back, and you be repaid. But when you give a feast, invite the poor, the maimed, the lame, the blind. And you will be blessed, because they cannot repay you; for you shall be repaid at the resurrection of the just'" (Luke 14:12-14).

Serving others!

"Yet if your brother is grieved because of your food, you are no longer walking in love. Do not destroy with your food the one for whom Christ died" (Romans 14:15).

Sensitivity to others!

"...with all lowliness and gentleness, with longsuffering, bearing with one another in love," (Ephesians 4:2).

Putting up with others!

"...but, speaking the truth in love, may grow up in all things into Him who is the head – Christ" (Ephesians 4:15).

Be honest with others!

"For out of much affliction and anguish of heart I wrote to you, with many tears, not that you should be grieved, but that you might know the love which I have so abundantly for you" (2 Corinthians 2:4).

Paul cried for those for whom Jesus died. That's how much he loved them. When was the last time you cried over a brother or sister in Christ because you loved them so much? This age is such a self-centered age. The only hope is you and your ability to love.

"And we urge you, brethren, to recognize those who labor among you, and are over you in the Lord and admonish you, and to esteem them very highly in love for their work's sake. Be at peace among yourselves" *(1 Thessalonians 5:12-13).*

The Bible tells us our spiritual leaders are worthy of double honor. I speak in hundreds of churches and I see the same thing everywhere: apathetic ministry because the people don't love their Pastors. They're there for what they can get from a church service. If they only realized that love will change the church into a place that will give them what they're looking for.

Our Pastors should be making a salary double the amount of what the members make. But most don't. Most barely scrape by. It's wrong. Where's the esteem the Lord is talking about?

Every Sunday I take a gift to my Pastors, usually something from the Farmer's Market, and if there is something I don't like about the church—I've never found a perfect church anyway—I keep it to myself and talk it over with the Holy Spirit. He's the only one who can do anything about it anyway.

"Let no one despise your youth, but be an example to the believers in word, in conduct, in love, in spirit, in faith, in purity" (1 Timothy 4:12).

"Flee also youthful lusts; but pursue righteousness, faith, love, peace with those who call on the Lord out of a pure heart" (2 Timothy 2:22).

Paul is talking to Timothy in those last two verses, instructing him in how to be a good Pastor. Pastors are also required to love. Love is like the engine that runs everything. Just like energy runs our physical world, love runs our spiritual world. Modify your behavior to be a lover of the Lord and a lover for the Lord.

THE LOVE REWARD

I was born again on a Sunday. Walking to church with my two children on a day following a rain, I relished the scent in the air, the sparkle on the leaves, the glisten of the pavement, when suddenly an audible voice spoke to me coming from somewhere just in front and above my head. I looked up.

"You've come a long way, Marty, but there's one more step you must take."

Instantly I knew to what the voice referred. Two months earlier I attended a prayer meeting with my aunt because of my terrible depression. Continuously I contemplated suicide so she pulled me to this evening meeting. While sitting in the circle of chairs arranged outside because of the heat, I closed my eyes and saw a bright, white light like a ball of fire larger than a man.

As I observed this phenomenon the figure of Jesus stepped out of the light, offered His hands and said, "Come to Me." Irresistibly I started to stand when the Pastor said 'Amen.' Now obligated to open my eyes, I discovered that what I thought took two minutes actually took two hours. I'd been mesmerized with Jesus for two hours!

I didn't get born again then. But He came home with me. He whispered to me day and night, loving words. On the Sunday in question I felt much better about myself than I had two months previously, so I responded to the audible voice, "What?"

"You have to say with your mouth that I am your Lord."

Rage rose up inside of me! No one was going to be my Lord but me! However, I knew if I didn't say 'yes' to this request, His wonderful presence would leave me. I stormed into church, threw myself into a back pew and pouted. When it was time for the congregation to go forward to take communion, I went up and knelt at the altar.

Looking at the cross irreverently I said, "Okay, Jesus, You are my Lord."

Something cold and nasty left my body by the bottom of my feet and something warm and wonderful seemed to come into my body from that cross and I've never been the same since! Love filled me up! God is love! Jesus is love! Holy Spirit is love! They all came to live inside me and They changed me!

Two days later I attended a ladies luncheon. The hostess wrapped a lovely present in an artistic display and put it in the center of the table as the door prize. I didn't know what was in the package but I knew it was mine. I knew I would win the drawing. And I did.

That was my first example of the love reward. Rummaging through my memory to tell you other examples, I find there are so many and they are so constant that my mind is flooded. Let me just give you a sampling from this last month of my life.

Friends invited me to accompany them to Israel on a Prayer Journey in November. I needed to decline because of finances, but a woman I had never seen before came to my book table after a certain service saying she had a message from the Lord for me. She said the Lord wanted me to know I would be going to Israel this fall, in November, and the trip would be paid for.

At my very next service, a workshop I did in the south of France, my hostess took up an offering from the twelve women attending. I expected about 100 Euros. Instead I received enough Euros to pay for my entire trip! I have my ticket and cash in hand for everything else! My hostess said, "I know these women! They don't have any money! Where did this offering come from?" It's part of the love reward.

A translator is transforming my book, *Destined for Healing*, into French. In there I say "Look at how much importance God puts on His Word." Then I quote Psalm 138:2. "For You have magnified Your Word above all Your Name."

She emailed to say she couldn't find that in the French Bible, what should she do? I checked my French Bible and indeed it wasn't there. I told her to take out the sentence and the Scripture. A few days later she emailed again saying the Lord woke her up in the middle of the night and had her research all her French Bibles. In one printed in 1978 she found it just as it was in English. So she put my text and the Scripture back in with a footnote explaining the quote.

To me this was as exciting as the Israel trip. God is involved in my work to the extent that He will wake up a translator and show her what to do. That's more love reward!

This month I went to Turkey. My denomination blessed its European missionaries with a retreat for a week. World Missions Ministries is definitely a love reward for me! When I first became a missionary I went under my Bible school's auspices. Their approach is that if God calls you, He'll provide everything you need. When I complained to the Lord that what I needed was relationship, encouragement, companionship, He directed me to Pentecostal Holiness and I have been blessed ever since.

Everything about that trip to Turkey smacked of the love reward. Since my flight left early I booked a hotel room the night before. When I checked in the attendant gave me a room for half the price quoted on the phone. The hotel kept my car so I didn't have to pay long term parking – exorbitant in France. Someone shared my taxi of 6 a.m. to the airport, half price again. And so it went throughout the trip.

These examples are just a glimpse into what I'm calling the love reward.

"...for the Father Himself loves you, because you have loved Me, and have believed that I came forth from God" (John 16:27).

Here are two conditions for receiving the love reward. First you are to love Jesus. You can't just know Him or know about Him. You have to love Him. And what's not to love in someone who died for you so that you would have eternal life! Second you have to believe that Jesus came forth or is a part of God. He's not just a Prophet, or just a Teacher. He's God.

"Jesus answered and said to him, 'If anyone loves Me, he will keep My word; and My Father will love him, and We will come to him and make Our home with him'" (John 14:23).

What is the 'word' of Jesus? To love one another as He has loved you. That's His only commandment. You know the Bible says He will never leave you nor forsake you, but He can sure be quiet in there. Practice anything contrary to His commandment and see what I mean. He doesn't withdraw; He just gets quiet.

"But if anyone loves God, this one is known by Him" (1 Corinthians 8:3).

I don't want God to just know about me. I want Him to know me. I want Him to call me by my name, which He does, only now that I'm born again He uses my birth name, Martha. I want Him to intimately know all the struggles in my life and to help me with them. I want to be known by Him! And, I want to know Him!

"that their hearts may be encouraged, being knit together in love, and attaining to all riches of the full assurance of understanding, to the knowledge of the mystery of God, both of the Father and of Christ," (Colossians 2:2).

This divine knowledge of knowing Him and Him knowing you is loaded with the love reward:

1. encouraged hearts. I need encouragement; don't you?

2. knitted to other believers in love. Commitment. Keith Moore says, "Where there is no commitment, there is no true love." This is really what keeps a church together – the love the members have for one another. People move from church to church looking for that love.

3. having all the riches involved in the full assurance of understanding. Don't you need understanding? Do you like being involved in things you don't understand? Don't you investigate and research until you find understanding? The love reward includes God giving you understanding.

4. the knowledge of the mystery of God, both of the Father and of Christ. The world has tried to explain this mystery in many of its carnal ways and always ends up deifying a man or humanizing God. But you, you have the love reward of the knowledge of this mystery! To someone outside it is foolishness because they don't understand, but to you it is knowledge from on high, from the Throne of God.

"Listen, my beloved brethren: Has God not chosen the poor of this world to be rich in faith and heirs of the kingdom which He promised to those who love Him?" (James 2:5).

James is using the word 'poor' in the relative sense. He's not speaking of finances; he's speaking of understanding and knowledge. Those who know they don't understand spiritual things and thereby come to the Lord acknowledging His superiority, receive love rewards. Such as:

1. rich in faith. There is faith and there is special faith. Special faith is a gift of the Holy Spirit. Special Faith brings on the thing you are having faith for. Our own faith is enough to please God,

but then He adds His gift of Special Faith and with that the only way you won't receive is if you stop believing.

2. heirs of the Kingdom. This gift is almost unimaginable. The Kingdom of God became your country when you were born again. In it are all treasures, the fulfillment of all promises, knowledge, understanding, wisdom, freedom and this Kingdom can only be entered by love. It's yours. The Bible says it belongs to you because you are a citizen. If given your authority, this Kingdom controls the life you live right now on earth.

"Love as brothers, be tenderhearted, be courteous; not returning evil for evil or reviling for reviling, but on the contrary blessing, knowing that you were called to this, that you may inherit a blessing. For He who would love life and see good days, let him refrain his tongue from evil and his lips from speaking deceit" (1 Peter 3:8b-10).

You can see, without a doubt, that it pays to love God. Now look at what the love reward is for loving your brothers and sisters in Christ. If we are tenderhearted and courteous, if we bless our brothers and sisters even when they treat us like dirt, we will inherit a blessing.

I don't know about you, but I do love life. I love to enjoy every day I live. How wonderful it is to wake up in the morning excited to see another day, knowing there are marvels waiting for me to discover! I like seeing good days.

Life is wonderful!

I'm not saying that's true because I've had a life of ease and everything has been done for me. Probably there are people like that; I just don't know them. Jesus couldn't exactly call you an overcomer if you didn't have anything to overcome and almost everybody, no I'd say everybody has something to overcome in life.

I'm saying life is wonderful because it is! Just by modifying your behavior to be a blessing instead of a cursing, you will be able to love life and see good days. Love God. Love Christians. That's what He is asking for.

"And whatever we ask we receive from Him, because we keep His commandments and do those things that are pleasing in His sight. And this is His commandment: that we should believe on the name of His Son Jesus Christ and love one another, as He gave us commandment" (1 John 3:22-23).

He's asking that you believe in Jesus, have full trust in Him, and that you love one another. If you do that – wow! how simple Christianity is – whatever you ask you receive from Him. The moment you ask, you receive. It may take time to manifest, but He will get it to you. What more could you possibly ask for? The ultimate rewards come from love.

"But as it is written: 'Eye has not seen, nor ear heard, nor have entered into the heart of man the things which God has prepared for those who love Him'" (1 Corinthians 2:9).

This is not a "pie in the sky" promise. This does not require your death. You already died. The moment you received Jesus as Lord your spirit man died and you received a new spirit with which you live in the Kingdom of God right now. Your eternal life started the moment you received that new spirit. So those things God has prepared also started with your new citizenship. All that's required is loving Him.

Let me ask a really simple question. Does He know you love Him? Do you tell Him every day? Does your behavior show Him that you love Him? Do your words show Him that you love Him? God's prepared the love reward, now it's up to you to give the love.

"But also for this very reason, giving all diligence, add to your faith virtue, to virtue knowledge, to knowledge self-control, to self-control perseverance, to perseverance godliness, to godliness brotherly kindness, and to brotherly kindness love. For if these things are yours and abound, you will be neither barren (useless) nor unfruitful in the knowledge of our Lord Jesus Christ. For he who lacks these things is shortsighted, even to blindness, and has forgotten that he was cleansed from his old sins. Therefore, brethren, be even more diligent to make your call and election sure, for if you do these things you will never stumble; for so an entrance will be supplied to you abundantly into the everlasting kingdom of our Lord and Savior Jesus Christ" (2 Peter 1:5-11).

This listing of eight duplicates the nine fruit of the Spirit, only missing joy and I would imagine joy is the experience you will have in the everlasting Kingdom of Jesus Christ. Galatians 5:22 begins the list with love and this passage ends the list with love. Love is the bookends of every spiritual blessing.

Personally I would like never to stumble again. Years ago I had bunions removed from my big toes. My surgeon chose to cut off my big toes, shorten them and put them back on again. Since then I stumble all the time because the big toe supplies the balance for the body. But stumbling in the issues of life is far worse and far more painful than a simple loss of stance as I quickly regain my physical composure. It doesn't come back so easily when I stumble in the issues of life.

This Scripture says if you conform to and establish love you will never stumble. It says you won't be useless in life; you'll have purpose. You won't be unfruitful; what you do will be productive and make a difference in the world. Isn't this what you really want? Isn't this so much better than being a couch potato and numbing your mind with senseless TV programs?

At the same time, don't be deceived. No one ever becomes famous for loving their brothers and sisters in Christ. But the rewards are great! Let me give you an example of a Christian family I know.

The father retired from being a farmer, his eldest son took over the farm. His other son opened a Garden Shop in their town. Farmers in California during this epoch borrowed money at the beginning of the year for seed, living expenses, farm expenses, etc., and at the end of the harvest they paid back the loan and kept the excess.

One year the eldest son borrowed $100,000. However, it was a dismal year for farming and not only he but every farmer experienced crop failure. The son could not pay back the $100,000. It meant he would lose the farm. The younger son had saved money from his successful shop to open another one so he gave that money to his brother and the father gave out of his savings to his son and thereby the eldest son paid back the loan.

Other farmers, however, had to sell their land. Developers moved right in on this choice location and built homes on the once fertile fields. His father was able to invest in some of this development and gained back much more than he gave his son. The youngest son opened more and more Garden Shops to meet the needs of all the new homeowners. All three have ended up quite wealthy and the family well intact because they loved each other enough to bear each other's burdens.

This example is how the Church should be behaving. Practice love. The love reward is phenomenal! Let me paint a picture for you of what I consider to be the greatest love reward of all.

"So continuing daily with one accord in the temple, and breaking bread from house to house, they ate their food with gladness and simplicity of heart, praising God and having

favor with all the people. And the Lord added to the church daily those who were being saved" (Acts 2:46-47).

Jesus, the farmer in James 5:7, is waiting for the last great harvest. It's going to be ginormous! (Okay, so I made up a word putting giant and enormous together. But how else can the last harvest of God be described?) Notice He is the one waiting! Everybody thinks we're waiting on Him. What's He waiting for? I believe the answer is love.

"Therefore be patient, brethren, until the coming of the Lord. See how the farmer waits for the precious fruit of the earth, waiting patiently for it until it receives the early and latter rain" (James 5:7).

My Pastors here in France are from Argentina. They were born again in the early days of the Argentinean revival. That revival is still going on. I question them all the time. Why Argentina? What was the catalyst? They said no one has come up with the answers to those questions.

Christians like to say prayer sparks revival and they always point to Wales or to Brownsville. Both of those fizzled after a couple of years. They were moves of God, not revivals. Revival brings a people back to its origins. Bars close. Society changes.

In the early 80s I went to a meeting in which Juan Carlos Ortiz preached. He spoke on the love commandment. Before moving to the United States he pastored a large church in Argentina and in his study of the Bible he discovered this love commandment, the Law of Christ. He challenged his church to follow that one command, to love one another as Christ loved them. He challenged them to make the world aware that they were Christians by how much love they poured out on their fellow Christians.

Asking the members to build houses for other members who did not have houses, he led the way. Juan Carlos discovered that his gardener, a member of the church, did not have a house while Juan Carlos had two, one for summer by the lake and one for winter in town. He said he didn't deny his family anything, but they agreed that they would give up certain spendings, like pizza delivery on a Friday night, in order to save the money for a house for the gardener. It took them two years. But Juan Carlos and his family built the house and gave it to the gardener, including the land.

Other members of the church, inspired by this effort, followed suit until everyone in the church owned their own home. Other churches picked up the mantle and did the same for their members. What was the result? Juan Carlos was expelled from Argentina! He was turning society upside down and politicians don't know what to do with that!

What was the other result? I'm convinced this is what triggered the great Argentina revival. Love was the spark and the fire has not died. Jesus is waiting for our fruit. What is our fruit? Love.

Let me give you one more long passage of Scripture. I would suggest you read this to yourself, and to your family, every night. I say night because if I want something to be impressed in my soul I read it just before going to sleep. But day time works as well. The important thing is to get it in your heart.

"Though I speak with the tongues of men and of angels, but have not love, I have become sounding brass or a clanging cymbal.

And though I have the gift of prophecy, and understand all mysteries and all knowledge, and though I have all faith, so that I could remove mountains, but have not love, I am nothing.

And though I bestow all my goods to feed the poor, and though I give my body to be burned, but have not love, it profits me nothing.

Love suffers long and is kind; love does not envy; love does not parade itself, is not puffed up;

...does not behave rudely, does not seek its own, is not provoked, thinks no evil;

...does not rejoice in iniquity, but rejoices in the truth;

...bears all things, believes all things, hopes all things, endures all things.

Marty Delmon

Love never fails. But whether there are prophecies, they will fall; whether there are tongues, they will cease; whether there is knowledge, it will vanish away.

For we know in part and we prophesy in part.

But when that which is perfect has come, then that which is in part will be done away.

When I was a child, I spoke as a child, I understood as a child, I thought as a child; but when I became a man, I put away childish things.

For now we see in a mirror, dimly, but then face to face. Now I know in part, but then I shall know just as I also am known.

And now abide faith, hope, love, these three; but the greatest of these is love" (1 Corinthians 13:1-13).

As a means of my saying goodbye, since it is the end of the book, let me join Paul in saying this:

"Finally, brethren, farewell. Become complete. Be of good comfort, be of one mind, live in peace; and the God of love and peace will be with you" (2 Corinthians 13:11).

Make up your mind, every day, that you are going to be a vessel of love that will tip yourself over and pour yourself out on every occasion, every person you possibly can. Be in competition with yourself. Can you love more than you did before? Can you love the enemy that is ripping you apart? Can you love someone who can't love back? Go for it! Be the epitome of love! Make your name great in the eyes of God by how much you love! You'll be amazed at the results.

MORE BOOKS by MARTY DELMON

SLEEPING WITH DEMONS
www.tatepublishing.com

Married to a man caught in the trap of sexual deviation, Maggie Dubois takes us on her lone journey through the dark valleys of one-sided marriage. Her passage through the somber alley of longing for love is a story that applies to us all.

Denying the existence of the problem, homosexuality, Maggie is ensnared in the conflict. The climax of the book comes when Maggie breaks through the veil of confusion to recognize the truth and confront the spiritual darkness. Exorcising the evil from her life, Maggie walks free.

"Lessons of Life" could well be a subtitle of this book as Maggie guilelessly shares her insights and revelations of what she discovers as she feels her way through the morass. Her discoveries liberate not only herself but her husband as well. Maggie's victory is everyone's victory: truth and freedom.

BURIED LIES
www.tatepublishing.com

No action evokes as much violent emotion and reaction as does incest. Murder, suicide, hatred, imprisonment, all things ugly in life evolve from this insidious trap set in a female child by her father. Journey with seven women as they confront their past, unearth the lies they have believed about themselves, replacing them with the  truth and see the changes made in their lives today. Against all odds, these seven overcame the most heinous of sins: sex forced upon them by Daddy.

Between the ages of 8 and 17 my stepfather perfunctorily raped me. At age 17, I confided in a girl friend and she encouraged me to confront him, asking why he would do such a thing. It never occurred to me I had the personal power to get him to stop, but when I followed her advice, he quit. The trauma stayed with me, however, coloring my future and damaging my potential until I received Jesus as my Lord.

The Holy Spirit led me into a prayer process in which Jesus helped me to uncover the lies I believed about myself because of what happened to me. The important part was that He planted the truth in me to replace those lies. It has made all the difference in my life.

Through the course of interviewing people for the stories I write for radio, I discovered that almost one woman out of two suffered what I suffered in my childhood. I have helped some to unearth the lies and believe the truth, but a book about it will reach far more women than I personally can reach. Therefore I have written Buried Lies.

BURIED LIES
COMPANION WORKBOOK

When I came to the Lord I carried a lot of baggage. My illegitimate birth, the continual raping by my stepfather between the ages of 8 and 17, my mother telling me I was too stupid to be a writer so I abandoned my passion, the self-sabotage I committed when I broke up with the love of my life because he was 'too good for me', and then the man I did marry, after ten years of marriage and two children, confessed he was gay.

The Lord gave me a prayer process to clear out the chaos in my life which came not because of all these things that happened to me, but because of the lies I believed about myself because of what happened. I called that book Buried Lies. When people read Buried Lies they asked me to do a workshop to lead them through the prayer process. I thought this to be good as it took me seven hours to complete my first process simply because the prayer is intensely focused and I wasn't accustomed to praying that thoroughly.

Then they asked for a workbook to take home so that they could continue to pull out lies and plant the truth. I decided to put the whole workshop into the workbook, leaving space at the end for them to go through the process themselves and journal about it.

My publisher came up with the best idea when he put the workbook on CD. He even allowed me to do the recording. Now people can take the workshop anywhere they want and the final of the four CDs leads the listener through the prayer process. There is one more prayer to go through which the Lord also gave me for the purpose of hearing Him more clearly. I call it 'The Garden'.

WILD CARD
www.tatepublishing.com

His dream…. Ron La Fave had charted his path and meticulously pursued it. Deflecting every distraction and breaking his own heart in the process, he persevered to the point of wounding his loved ones as he doggedly attained the success that powered his dreams.

But, Ron failed to recognize the reality of evil. Dreams can be sabotaged from within, yet the threat from without comes like a sidewinder. One strike, one puncture and the aspiration deflates like a party balloon flailing wildly about the room.

Wherever he turned, the serpent hoisted its evil head. His Board of Directors threw him out; his wife left; his mentor disowned him; his bank accounts closed; his reputation tanked and the industry blackballed him. Left with nothing, he retreated to Jackson Hole.

Counting on the mountains to restore him, he hid in the Tetons. However, a certain Presence wouldn't leave. Ron found himself grappling with distractions he could not deflect and instead of the peace he sought, he tormentedly confronted good and evil.

Learning to accept the one and reject the other, a spiritual path opened which revealed success beyond his wildest dreams. Suddenly, every conflict in life resolved itself. His broken heart healed as well as those of his loved ones. Learning the art of service, against which the serpent has no power, Ron became a man who makes a difference.

In Wild Card you will find your own spiritual path. Choose it. Change your life.

DESTINED FOR SUCCESS
www.rpjandco.com

Isaiah foretold the cross, the price Jesus would pay and the benefits we would receive. He mentioned prosperity. "The chastisement of our prosperity was upon Him," Is 53:5. The Hebrew word is SHALOM! While the translators used the word 'peace' in this verse, both prosperity and peace are the meanings of SHALOM. The two words are interchangeable. Can you have peace without prosperity? Doesn't prosperity bring peace? Jesus paid for you to have prosperity. It's a new-birth right. **Destined for Success** defines that prosperity and directs you to the path to receive it. SHALOM!

DESTINED FOR HEALING
www.rpjandco.com

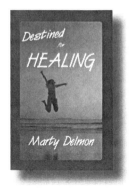

All around the author sees unnecessary sickness and pain. She sees people trying to explain away their failure at being healed. The author knows from personal experience the triumph of overcoming the disease of the body and wanted to share the knowledge she's gained. May the Body of Christ truly be transformed by accepting the healing that Jesus bought for us with His body.

Soon to be released...
DESTINED FOR FAITH
www.rpjandco.com

What is it that makes a Christian's life different from that of a person who doesn't believe in Jesus Christ the Son of God? Gosh, you may say, where do I begin? There can be a long list, I know, but it really boils down to one thing. We trust God.

You have to trust God even to get saved. You have to trust God to forgive you. That's where most Christians stop, when it's really where Christians should begin. The seed of faith that you are given at your new birth is the most powerful servant possible. I don't care what the Bible has promised you, every promise in there is waiting to be given to you, in this life here on earth, by your servant, Faith.

The disciples wanted more of this stuff. When they saw how faith made Jesus walk on water or dry up a fig tree or bring people back from the dead or heal people or pay taxes they wanted that. Jesus said we can have more and do more than He ever did. How? By putting our faith to work. It's a learning process and it's written down in this book so you can read and put it into practice.

Some things remain a mystery until the time has come for the promise to be fulfilled. It's time for Faith. It's time for united faith in the Body of Christ. God is answering faith. It's been a long time coming, but now the majority of the Church is ready to read and run with the vision – through Faith which conquers the world!

A Message from the Author

You are perfect you. No one can be more perfectly you than you are. God made you completely unique so there can be no duplicate, no substitute. He made you for Himself and He knows you because there is nobody else like you.

Yes, you have two natures. When the sperm from your father joined the egg from your mother, one nature came into being which governs your body and your soul. This nature is a fallen one, inherited from all your generations back to the original sin.

When that sperm and egg became one, more was created than a stem cell. At conception God breathed into you your spirit which is your divine nature, a portion of the Spirit of God. God is Love and God is Light. Your spirit is made of love and light.

About the age of twelve a certain portion of your brain began its appointed time of development: the ability to reason and make decisions on your own. You, like everyone else, learned you could choose between good and evil – not just be naughty or nice – but to choose evil and you found you could, at least for awhile, live with its consequences. Or you could choose good and receive its gracious and glorious rewards.

Unfortunately, choosing evil overrode your conscience, the gateway to your spirit. You seared your conscience and the door between the fallen nature and the divine nature stood open like a rusty gate. Sadly, your divine nature became corrupt like your fallen nature.

You can't just clean up a corrupt spirit; you have to exchange it for a new one. How is that possible? God already gave you your portion of His Spirit. So how do you get another one? You accept the gift of Jesus Christ. He came to take your place, to pay for what you did wrong, to erase your sins and give you a portion of His Spirit.

He blew on His disciples, they received His Spirit and became born again. He continues to breathe on new believers today. Whenever anyone says, "Jesus, I have sinned against You, Your Father and the Kingdom of God..." (see the rest of this prayer at the end of this discourse) and sincerely means it, Jesus will give him or her a new spirit.

You can be born again. Once you have received your new birth you can get your soul saved and your body will follow suit because your body does whatever your soul tells it to do. How do you get your soul saved? Obeying the Spirit of God with a willing heart one step at a time cleans up your soul and works your salvation from the inside, where your spirit man is, through the soul, your mind, emotions and will, to the outside to be expressed in your body.

Only those who receive Jesus as Lord today will live tomorrow in the Kingdom of God forever. Those who do not receive Him as their Lord will spend eternity in the kingdom of darkness. Choose today. Start your Eternal Life by giving yourself to Jesus and making Him your Lord. Love and Light will once again reside in your new spirit and He will give you His abundant life.

THE SINNER'S PRAYER

Jesus, I have sinned against You, Your Father and the Kingdom of God. I've made a mess of things by trying to run my own life and running away from you. Please forgive me. Please apply the blood You so painfully shed to pay for my sins to my spirit, soul and body. I receive You now, Jesus, as my Savior, my Lord, my best Friend, my Master and my Commander in Chief. I will love You, I will serve You, I will honor You, I will proclaim You all the days of my life and I will live with You for eternity in Heaven, the Kingdom of Love. Thank You, Jesus! I am Yours! Amen.

About the Publisher

In 2004, the Spirit of God birthed RPJ & Company according to Romans 14:17.

RPJ & Company, Inc. began publishing Christian books for pastors, leaders, ministers, missionaries, and others with a message to help the Body of Christ. Our published books continue to empower, inspire and motivate people to aspire to a higher level of understanding through the written word.

Our company is dedicated to assisting those individuals who desire to publish Christian books that are uplifting, inspiring and self-help in nature. We also offer assistance for those who would like to self-publish.

The special service that we provide is customized, quality layout and design for every client. This gives every new author a chance at becoming successfully-published. For every book, we offer exposure and a worldwide presence to help the book and the author become discovered!

"As an author and publisher, I can guide you through the steps of creating, editing, proofreading and providing you with a professional layout and design for any printed item, one you'll be proud to call your own."

- Kathleen Schubitz
Founder and CEO

RPJ & COMPANY, INC.
"Where quality and excellence meet face to face!"

www.store.rpjandco.com